THE ART OF COMMUNICATING LOVE TO YOUR PARTNER

The Art of Communicating Love To Your Partner

MICHAEL & CAROLYN BYRD

Byrd Family Books

The Art of COMMUNICATING LOVE TO YOUR PARTNER

ALL RIGHTS RESERVED. No part of this book or ebook may be modified or altered in any form whatsoever, electronic, or mechanical, including photocopying, recording, or by any informational storage or retrieval system without express written, dated and signed permission from the author.

Copyright © 2023 Mike and Carol Byrd

Table of Contents

Introduction

Chapter 1
Listening

Chapter 2
Talking

Chapter 3
Body Language

Chapter 4
Daily Habits

Conclusion

THE ART OF COMMUNICATING LOVE TO YOUR PARTNER ~ 3

Introduction

Effective communication is essential for cultivating a thriving and nourishing relationship. However, it can often pose challenges to articulate thoughts and emotions in a gentle and compassionate manner.

Many couples find it challenging to engage in loving and thoughtful communication, as they navigate the demands of daily life and the pressures of maintaining a healthy relationship. However, by cultivating deep listening, compassion, and vulnerability, it is possible to create a space of intimacy and connection where both partners can share their feelings and needs without fear or judgment. Through intentional dialogue and a commitment to mutual understanding, couples can transform their communication patterns and forge a path towards greater love and fulfillment.

Loving communication can be integrated into listening, talking, body language, daily habits, and other activities.

Discover how to utilize all these diverse forms of communication to deepen your relationship and cultivate a more exultant and enriching love.

> *"Communication is the art of painting a picture with words. When it comes to love, the canvas is your partner's heart, and the brush is your willingness to express."*
> *- Mike & Carol Byrd*

Chapter 1

Listening

When engaging in communication with your partner, the art of listening is of utmost importance, even superseding the act of speaking itself. It is imperative that you lend your ears with great care and attentiveness to your beloved counterpart.

Unfortunately, it is oftentimes easier to give a speech than tender our undivided attention to one another.

Many couples develop habitual patterns in their conversations, such as disconnecting from one another by tuning out or nodding in agreement without truly listening. These small behaviors of inattention may seem insignificant in the moment, but over time they can accumulate and create a distance between partners.

Unfortunately, these actions can have dire consequences for the relationship.

Instead of treating conversations as just mere exchanges of words, one can utilize them to strengthen their relationship by expressing their love and affection through them.

"In order to demonstrate your love through listening, consider implementing the following tactics:"

When your partner is speaking, direct your eyes towards them. Not only will this action illustrate your undivided attention, but it also creates a positive, respectful, and complimentary dynamic - even when you're not the one speaking.

To truly engage in a meaningful conversation, one must practice the art of active listening. This skilled approach to listening reveals a deep level of engagement in the discourse at hand.

There are many forms of active listening that can be employed.

- Examples of active listening can include a nod of the head, asserting your agreement, or even posing thoughtful questions to clarify the meaning behind one's statements

It is essential to demonstrate comprehension in any conversation. Often, even a simple nod or smile suffices, but occasionally, it may be helpful to continue the dialogue and offer advice or tips.

Interruptions are detrimental to effective communication. Whether it be a ringing phone or disrupting the speaker while they are speaking, interruptions are exasperating and weaken the flow of communication.

- Turn off your phones and other devices while you're listening to your partner.
- It is essential to prioritize conversations above all else. Through meaningful and intentional communication, we can foster deep connections, gain new insights, and expand our awareness. By placing importance on meaningful conversations, we begin to transcend

the monotony of everyday life and explore the richness of our shared human experience.

Show how much you care by the way you listen. Your partner will notice the loving difference

Chapter 2

Talking

The way in which you communicate with your partner holds immense influence over your relationship. From casual chit-chat to affectionate nicknames, the sound of your voice holds great power.

Initially, couples can express their love through engaging conversations; however, as relationships progress, the words of affection may wane. But it is possible to maintain such a loving connection through verbal communication. Don't allow love to slip away during a simple conversation!

CONSIDER THESE TIPS FOR KEEPING YOUR LOVE ALIVE:

Don't discount the power of small talk.

Although deep and meaningful conversations are important, there are moments when light chatter can effectively express affection.

- Small talk offers a comfortable means of initiating a dialogue with your partner, discussing anything from work-related topics to the vagaries of the weather. By exchanging information with one another, you demonstrate your continued affection and regard for each other.

Sharing even mundane details of your life with someone can deepen your emotional connection and strengthen the bonds between you.

Every lover who seeks to maintain and grow a prosperous relationship must never forget to utilize affectionate and caring language. The employment of loving terms and endearing expressions can significantly impact and strengthen the bond between two partners.

- Using terms of endearment or adorable pet names is one possibility. This method is an effective tool for establishing a sense of warmth and intimacy while also contributing to a more imaginative and dynamic text.

It's important to consistently communicate affection in any long-term relationship. A common mistake some couples make is forgetting to express their love for one another. Make a point of telling your partner how much they mean to you. This simple act can keep the love and passion alive for years to come.

- Although there are myriad ways to express love, it is vital to vocalize the words "I love you" to your partner. This verbal commitment serves as a form of reassurance and a reminder of the powerful bond you share.

Express yourself with love. In difficult conversations, it is not uncommon for emotions such as anger and resentment to surface. However, it is crucial to actively resist succumbing to these feelings.

- Choose words with care and kindness when communicating with your partner. Strive to express yourself in a way that uplifts and encourages them, rather than tearing them down. Remember that your words hold power, and with grace and compassion, you can strengthen the bond between you and your beloved.
- As you engage in conversation with your partner, take a moment to consider how they will feel after hearing what you have to say. It is important to craft your words with care and convey your message in a compassionate and empathetic manner. By doing so, you can deepen your connection and foster greater understanding between you and your partner.
- Do not allow the intensity of anger and the fervor of the moment to obstruct your ability to make sound decisions.
- Sometimes, it can be beneficial to take a step back or go for a refreshing walk during a heated discussion. When you

return, choose words that still convey thoughts of affection.

- In a loving relationship, the manner in which you express yourself carries great significance. It is crucial to communicate your love through affirming words each day with exquisite delicacy, depth, and devotion.

"Words possess great power; choosing to speak words of love daily within our homes provides an atmosphere that nurtures growth and longevity."
-Mike and Carol Byrd

Chapter 3
Body Language

"Are you attuned to the subtleties of your partner's physical expression? As they move and gesture, do you observe and interpret the language of their body? Heightened awareness of nonverbal communication can enrich your relationship, deepening your intimacy and strengthening your connection. Through attentiveness to the unspoken cues of your beloved, you can develop a profound understanding and appreciation for their being."

Your body language is another way to show love in a relationship. Whether you use your eyes or a smile, the subtle things can express love.

Your body language is important to your partner. They can pick up on unverbalized emotions from your body language, so make it count!

Try implementing these tips to convey affection through your physical cues:

One key aspect to improving communication with your partner is to focus on their eyes. Are you truly present in the moment, making eye contact and actively listening, or are you distracted by the world around you?

By choosing to fully engage and look into your partner's eyes, you are creating a deeper connection and showing them the respect and attention, they deserve. Don't let technology or other distractions prevent you from fully connecting with your loved one.

- Researchers have discovered that partners who gaze intently into one another's eyes tend to have stronger and more fulfilling relationships. Therefore, it is crucial to make direct eye contact with your partner while both speaking and listening to them.

- One should strive to maintain eye contact and avoid becoming distracted by their surroundings while engaged in conversation.
- If you happen to avert your gaze while your loved one is speaking, they may assume that you are disinterested in the conversation, or in them, altogether.

1. Smile. It is undoubtedly important to smile at appropriate times, and yet, many couples tend to overlook its significance entirely. However, this seemingly simple gesture carries with it a world of significance.

   - Remember that the simplicity of a smile extends beyond its power to communicate positivity. Recent research has revealed that smiling can bolster your immune system and enhance your mood, making it a small yet potent gift to yourself.

2. Face your partner. As you engage in conversation, be sure to maintain eye contact and face one another, thereby demonstrating your attentive interest and respect for their personhood.

- Demonstrate your attentiveness by leaning forward during their discourse. This not only displays your concern but also signifies that you're actively engaged in the conversation.

3. Other body language. Incorporate these actions into your body language to effectively convey your love.

- During your conversation, make sure to affirm your understanding by nodding at appropriate moments.
- Directing your feet towards your partner not only demonstrates keen interest, but it also leads the body in that direction. This simple yet powerful gesture can convey a wide range of emotions without ever speaking a word.
- To enhance your communication skills, it's best to avoid crossing your arms as it may convey defensiveness and negativity. A study shows that individuals who do so are less likely to retain information from a conversation.

- In moments of hardship or deep emotion, holding your partner's hands can serve as a powerful expression of your love and support. Allow the warmth and energy to flow between your palms, connecting you in a deeper, more profound way. Let your eyes meet, and in that silent exchange, let your love speak volumes.

Mastering the art of nonverbal communication is an essential attribute to fostering a healthy relationship. Incorporate these expert body language techniques into your daily routine to elevate your connection to an unparalleled level of intimacy and love.

> *The increasing prevalence of electronic devices is causing us to lose our ability to connect with each other on a deeper level. We are losing our proficiency in social skills, and with it, the ability to read a person's mood and body language, and to exercise the*

patience necessary to make or press a point at the right moment. Daily human connection is a crucial component of community life and living together, and as we become more reliant on technology, we are becoming increasingly dehumanized.

- Mike and Carol Byrd

Chapter 4

Daily Habits

How do you express your love through daily rituals and practices?

The daily rituals of a relationship hold the power to make a monumental impact, whether it's by way of serving your partner their first cup of coffee each morning or meticulously folding their clothes in a certain way that they prefer.

Have you ever reflected on how your daily routines impact your significant other?

The following habits will magnify and deepen the love flourishing within your relationship:

1. Continue to write love notes, for they

are a timeless and cherished way to convey your affection. Despite the changing tides of modernity, the enduring power of a heartfelt letter remains unchanged. Never underestimate the power of the written word in expressing your deepest emotions.

- Write a short love note on a sticky note.
- A tender and heartfelt gesture can be conveyed through a simple yet meaningful email or social media post. The act of writing it on fancy paper is not necessary to convey its depth of feeling.
- Even a loving text message can brighten your partner's day.

Make date night part of the schedule. Even if an enchanting evening out with your beloved may not be a weekly tradition, making it a regular part of your lifestyle is still possible and rewarding.

- Incorporating at least one evening of

intimate and romantic pleasure into your timetable per month may seem like a small and trivial detail, but it can work wonders for you and your partner's connection.
- Date night is the perfect opportunity to practice your loving communication and reconnect.
- Keep in mind that date night need not be lavish or costly. A tranquil and modest dinner at home or a movie night cuddled up on the sofa make for exquisite date excursions. You may also explore museums, art galleries, or attend a live theatrical performance, even a complimentary one.

Sharing small gifts. Although gifts are often expected on holidays and birthdays, you can share smaller ones throughout the year.

- Let us ponder the act of gifting each other with small yet significant presents more regularly, as a means of fostering deeper connections and enriching our lives.

- Consider presenting your partner with a thoughtful and practical token rather than a costly trinket. Perhaps, a charming set of journals or a high-quality pen may pleasure the interest of an avid writer.
- Even a photograph of you and your partner in a new frame can be a gift.

Share chores. One of the biggest complaints from couples is housework and sharing chores.

- You can express your affection by performing tasks proactively, without necessitating reminders.
- You can also lend a hand by assuming your significant other's portion of the household duties.
- It can be exhausting and disconnecting for a relationship when one individual takes on an unequal amount of household duties. Feelings of frustration and

bitterness can arise, while simultaneously experiencing increased fatigue.

Add more joy and laughter. Adding humor to your interactions can enhance your connection with others, from sharing witty jokes to enjoying humorous films together.

- By incorporating more joyful and laughter-filled moments into your relationship, you'll notice a greater sense of buoyancy and resilience as you relish in the time spent alongside your beloved.
- Try to add more humor to your daily interactions.
  Give foot rubs and massages. Your partner will deeply appreciate this gesture after a tiresome day at work or at home.
- Foot rubs and massages are free and an easy way to show you care.
- They are great romantic gestures that don't require a lot of planning or time.

Spend more time together. Every fleeting moment need not always be meticulously plotted and strategized.

- Concentrate on dedicating additional time to each other every day, and experience and incredible sense of interconnectedness that blossoms into a profound and unbreakable bond.
- You need not always plan a grand occasion to spend time together. It is in the ordinary moments - where you share meals or enjoy a quiet read together - that intimate connections are truly fostered.
- Snuggle together on the couch, go through paperwork together, or watch a show on TV.

The key is to be with each other and just enjoy each other's company.

Your daily routines have a significant impact on quality of your communication with your beloved. Get creative and incorporate your own unique ideas, discovering habits that create intimacy and closeness. Make it a habit to show your affection each day, as you interact with each other in your daily routines.

> *"Love is nourished through the power of imagination, through which we become wiser than we know, better than we feel, nobler than we are. It is through this power alone that we are able to comprehend life in its entirety, and truly understand others in both their true and ideal form. Only that which is exquisite and delicately crafted is able to satiate the hunger of love."*
> *- Mike and Carol Byrd*

Conclusion

When endeavoring to cultivate a robust and thriving relationship with your partner, it is crucial that loving communication serves as a cornerstone. Each word and act have the potential to convey affection. Every moment, from day-to-day routines to listening habits, affords the opportunity to express your devotion to your beloved.

Keep in mind that loving communication takes practice, so it may not happen in one day. **Have fun as you practice and try new ideas together!**

Over time, employing endearing expressions and benevolent deeds will gradually permeate your manner of expression. Your emotional connection will enhance as you communicate your affection in these manners.

> *The felicitous union of two souls, entwined in a sacred bond that transcends time and space, is a sublime and enchanting experience.*
> *- Mike and Carol Byrd*

www.ingramcontent.com/pod-product-compliance
Lightning Source LLC
Chambersburg PA
CBHW050450010526
44118CB00013B/1766